John Winslow

The battle of Lexington as looked at in London before

Chief-Justice Mansfield and a jury in the trial of John Horne

John Winslow

The battle of Lexington as looked at in London before Chief-Justice Mansfield and a jury in the trial of John Horne

ISBN/EAN: 9783337223946

Hergestellt in Europa, USA, Kanada, Australien, Japan

Cover: Foto ©ninafisch / pixelio.de

Weitere Bücher finden Sie auf **www.hansebooks.com**

Publications of the New York Society of the
Order of the Founders and Patriots of America

No. 2.

The Battle of Lexington

As looked at in London before
Chief-Justice Mansfield and a jury
in the trial of John Horne, Esq.,
for libel on the British Government

By Hon. John Winslow

Read before the New York
Society of the Order of the
Founders and Patriots of
America, May 13th, 1897

PREFACE.

The Order of the Founders and Patriots of America, is an Historical and Patriotic Society, consisting of descendants of those who, within the first fifty years after the settlement of Jamestown, came to and settled in the eight colonies, which afterwards became parts of the United States. Its members are also required to show that their intermediate ancestors of the Revolutionary period adhered as patriots to the cause of the Colonies. In the month of February, 1896, a few gentlemen met in the Astor House, in New York City, and took the preliminary formal steps toward the formation of the Order. On the 16th day of March, 1896, nine of those persons, namely: Edward N. G. Greene, Howard S. Robbins, Howard Marshall, Henry L. Morris, John Quincy Adams, Ralph E. Prime, Charles W. B. Wilkinson, Henry Hall and William W. Goodrich, met and founded the Order, and executed the Certificate of Incorporation of the New York Society. A plan of organization of the Order, with a general Constitution and By-Laws for the Order, was prepared, and on the 17th day of April, 1896, was adopted by the New York Society. The latter then consisted of seventy-eight gentlemen, whose eligibility had been examined, and who had been invited by the Founders of the Order to join them as Charter Members, and participate in the formal organization.

The plan embraced an Order, consisting of State Societies and Chapters, having a central representative body called the General Court. Since the organization of the Order, and of the New York State Society, societies have also been formed in New Jersey, Connecticut, Pennsylvania and Massachusetts, and Chapters of the New State Society have been created in Albany and Syracuse.

The first Governor of the New York Society was Col. Frederick Dent Grant, who was succeeded in turn by Col. Ralph Earl Prime, and he, in turn, by the incumbent, Hon. William Winton Goodrich.

The Officers of the New York Society for 1897-8 are as follows :

OFFICERS:

Hon. WILLIAM WINTON GOODRICH, Governor, . Brooklyn
CHARLES ALBERT HOYT, Deputy-Governor, . Brooklyn
MATTHEW HINMAN, Treasurer, 359 Broadway, New York City
HENRY LINCOLN MORRIS, Secretary,
253 Broadway, New York City
SAMUEL VICTOR CONSTANT, States-Attorney.
New York City
Col. LEWIS CHEESMAN HOPKINS, Registrar,
66 Broadway, New York City
GEORGE ROGERS HOWELL, Historian, . . . Albany
Rev. DANIEL FREDERICK WARREN, D. D., Chaplain,
Jersey City Heights, N. J.

COUNCILORS:

ONE YEAR.
CLARENCE LYMAN COLLINS, . New York City
Maj. ROBERT EMMET HOPKINS, . Tarrytown
WALTER STUEBEN CARTER, Brooklyn

TWO YEARS.
Gen. FERDINAND PINNEY EARLE, New York City
GEORGE CLINTON BATCHELLER. New York City
STEPHEN MOTT WRIGHT. . New York City

THREE YEARS.
Hon. JOHN WINSLOW, . . Brooklyn
JONAS HAPGOOD BROOKS, . Albany
Gen. STEWART L. WOODFORD, New York City

In the month of March, 1897, the New York Society invited the Hon. John Winslow, an associate of the Order, to read before the Society a paper on the legal aspects of the Battle of Lexington, as viewed in England at the time. He cheerfully acceded to the request, and was prepared to read his paper at the annual meeting held on the anniversary of that battle, but the circumstances were such that the reading was postponed to a special social meeting held at the Windsor Hotel, in New York City, on the evening of Thursday, the 13th day of May, 1897. The paper was regarded as a work of so much general interest and importance as to demand publication, and the Council of the New York Society appointed "a committee, consisting of Col. Ralph E. Prime and Edward Hagaman Hall, to request our associate, Hon. John Winslow, to furnish a copy of his paper (on the legal aspects of the Battle of Lexington) for publication by our Society, and that this committee, in conjunction with the

4

regular Printing Committee, have the paper published and distributed."

Pursuant to the direction of the Council, the following correspondence ensued :

63 Hawthorne Avenue,

YONKERS, N. Y., June 23rd, 1897.

HON. JOHN WINSLOW:

DEAR SIR :—It gives me great pleasure to inform you, that it is the earnest desire of the Council of the New York Society of the Order of the Founders and Patriots of America, that you would consent to the publication, as one of our historical papers, of your paper on the legal aspects of the Battle of Lexington, etc., recently read by you before that Society, at a social meeting held at the Windsor Hotel. I hope this will meet your pleasure.

In furtherance of such measure, the Council appointed a committee, consisting of the undersigned and Mr. Edward Hagaman Hall, to request your consent to the publication, and to ask of you a copy of the paper to be so published.

We regard the subject matter of more than historical interest, and do not fail to recognize the fact that it will also be of great interest to the members of the legal profession. Hence we have in mind the issue of such a number of copies as will not only supply the members of our Society, but the public libraries, and also all those of your profession and mine who shall desire it.

The Committee trusts that you will favorably answer the desire expressed.

Assuring you of my own sincere regard, I beg to assure you also of the unaffected regard of your associates.

For the Committee,

Yours, etc.,

(Signed)   RALPH E. PRIME.

BROOKLYN, N. Y., June 24th, 1897.

DEAR COL. R. E. PRIME:

Referring to your kind and appreciative letter of the 23rd inst., I infer that the Council ask consent for the publication of my Lexington-London paper because, among other reasons, they believe it will be of service to our Society as a part of its proper work. This alone is sufficient to induce me to comply with the request.

If I had known how much of time and research the paper would require, I might not, with other pressing engagements. have had courage for the work. The subject, I believe. has never before been presented as illustrative of the American Revolution, and of the view taken of it by British jurists.

Very respectfully and truly yours,

(Signed)   JOHN WINSLOW.

5

THE BATTLE OF LEXINGTON, as looked at in London, in the trial of John Horne, Esquire, before Chief Justice Mansfield and a jury, for libel on the British Government, is the subject to which your attention is called. It is easy enough for us, Americans, descendants of Revolutionary patriots, to see the battle with admiring eyes and grateful hearts. Some of us, perhaps, never stop to think, or care, how the thing appeared in London. While we look with reverence on the monuments at Lexington and Concord and Bunker Hill, it is not apt to occur to us that in London, and all Britain, our fathers appeared to be the most irreverent set of men that ever harassed a crown. It may be of some use, then, to see ourselves as others across the Atlantic saw us in the time of the Revolution. We may do so without in the least conceding anything to the credit of the British statesmen who advised the attempt of Great Britain to crush the North American Colonies. But, in looking at the other side, as it appears in the noted trial of John Horne, Esq., we may possibly gain a larger view of what was involved in the struggle of the Revolution; or, at least, we may see more clearly the environments of the time, and why the achievements of our fathers seemed glorious to them, and do to us, and why, to the great men who controlled the British Government, the breaking away of the Colonies seemed one of the saddest chapters in history. We shall also find in this trial a significant chapter in the history of the long struggle for freedom of thought and speech in the nations not considered barbaric, more especially among English speaking people. We shall see that the treatment accorded Mr. Horne by his government in the last quarter of the eighteenth century, was mild and humane compared with the drastic judgments in similar cases inflicted early in the seventeenth century, under the reign of the Stuarts, by their satellites, such as the Twelve Judges. Yet Lord Brougham, who was born about the time Horne was tried, saw and said, near the middle of the nineteenth century, that Horne's punishment was an outrage upon the rights of personal freedom of opinion, thus showing the progressive history of what now to us seems axiomatic touching personal liberty. Some one has said that, in civilized nations, the most important of human affairs sooner or later get before a court and jury. And so it will be seen that the principles and leading causes of the Revolution came to be considered by Lord Mansfield and a jury in the trial of Horne. The battles of Lexington and Concord were practically one battle. The objective on the part of the British was at least two-fold ; it was to seize some army stores in Concord, and also to seize two distinguished gentlemen, Samuel Adams and John Hancock, who were with Rev. Jonas Clark at Lexington, and were members of the Provincial Congress at Concord which had adjourned four days before the battle. The intended seizure was a failure.

The defendant's name in the trial for libel is John Horne, Esq., but in later life he was known as John Horne Tooke. This change of name is explained by the fact that, in resisting with much ability an enclosure bill pending in the Commons, he gained the favor of Mr. Tooke, of Purley, who said he would make him his heir, and so, in 1782, Horne changed his name to Tooke as a token of esteem for his friend and patron, and received about 8,000 pounds from his property. But, inasmuch as in the trial under consideration he was known as John Horne, Esq., he will be so referred to in this paper. Horne, who was well known as a leader in politics, and a philologist, was born in Westminster in 1736, and died in 1812. His father, a man of means, gave his son good opportunities for education at Westminster School, at Eton, and Cambridge University. Against his wish, but in obedience to his father, he took orders and was a curate in Kent. Having a strong liking for the law, he entered, in 1756, as a student at the Middle Temple, but soon after returned to the Church. Three years later he traveled on the continent. In 1765 he began his political life, writing pamphlets on public questions, and soon became intimate with Wilkes, the famous politician. He was active in supporting the election of Wilkes from Middlesex. In 1769 he was one of the founders of the society for supporting the Bill of Rights ; soon after he became involved in quarrels with Wilkes which impaired his popularity. After considerable opposition he received, in 1771, his degree of M.A. from Cambridge In 1773 he resigned his living, with the intention of studying law.

Horne bitterly opposed the British policy toward the American Colonies, and in the course of his opposition he wrote the famous advertisement which led to the accusation, by the information of the Attorney-General, Lord Thurlow, of libel on the King and Government.

Lord Mansfield, early in the trial, referred to the battle of Lexington as "the occasion at Lexington," but later took a graver view. The descriptive lines of Humphrey, who was regarded by his cotemporaries as more especially the poet of the Revolution, reflected the colonial view:

" As when dark clouds from Andes towering head,
" Roll down the skies and 'round th' horizon spread,
" With thunders fraught, the blackening tempest sails,
"And bursts tremendous o'er Peruvian vales—
"So broke the storm on Concord's fatal plain."

"Then the shrill trumpet echoed from afar,
" And sudden blazed the wasting flame of war,
" From State to State, swift flew the dire alarms,
" And ardent youths impetuous rushed to arms."

When the news of the battle of Lexington reached London, Horne was aroused, and denounced the attack made by General Gage, as murder, and proposed a subscription of 100 pounds, to be paid to Dr. Franklin for the American widows and orphans of the troops at Lexington and Concord.

The standing of Horne as a political critic is seen in the fact that the name of John Horne Tooke appears in the long list of eminent names suspected of the authorship of the " Letters of Junius." To have been thus suspected was a high tribute to Horne's intellectual force. It is not so easy now to comprehend the tremendous impression made by Junius as it was for his cotemporaries. To help in this respect, let us listen in the House of Commons to Burke, who thus graphically referred to it :

" How comes this Junius to have broke through the cobwebs of the law, and to range uncontrolled, unpunished through the land? The myrmidons of the court have been long, and are still, pursuing him in vain. They will not spend their time upon me or you. No, they disdain such vermin, when the mighty boar of the forest, that has broke through all their toils, is before them. But what will all their efforts avail? No sooner has he wounded one than he lays down another dead at his feet. For my part, when I saw his attack upon the King, I own my blood ran cold. I thought he had ventured too far, and there was an end of his triumph. Not that he had not asserted many truths, but while I expected in this daring flight his ruin and fall, behold him rising still higher and coming down souse upon the two Houses of Parliament. Yes, he did make for his quarry, and you still bleed from the wounds of his talons ; you crouched, and still crouch beneath his rage. Nor has he dreaded the terrors of your brow, sir; he has attacked even you—he has, and I believe you have no reason to triumph in the encounter. In short, after carrying away our royal eagle in his pounces, and dashing him against a rock, he has laid you prostrate. King, Lords and Commons are but the sport of his fury."

To have been supposed to be Junius, who could do such destructive work and send consternation among the leading British publicists, was a fine tribute to Horne. One of the reasons that led some to think that Horne was Junius was his bitter attacks upon Mansfield. Mansfield, and other legal advisers of the crown, labored assiduously to find how this " boar of the forest," as Burke called him, could be brought to punishment. Burke himself was once charged with being the mysterious author, but denied it in the House of Commons.

In about 1794, the Hon. John A. Graham, then a scholarly member of the New York bar, having occasion to visit England on ecclesiastical business for the Episcopal Convention of Vermont, met, as he tells us, many eminent men, including Horne, in whom he became much interested. Graham became impressed, as others were, that Horne was Junius. After his return to America, Mr. Graham studied quite elaborately Horne's style of expression and thought and animus on public questions, and thus became more thoroughly convinced that Horne was the mysterious writer. In 1828 Mr. Graham published a book on the subject, giving his reasons in detail for his conclusion. In this book he speaks of his departed friend in cordial terms and with great respect, and says of him : "he now stands '*clarum et venerabile nomen.*'" In the course of his argument Graham says: "His genius was transcendent, his talents of the first order, his struggles for liberty sincere, his privations and sufferings great, and his patriotism was undoubted." In another connection Graham refers to Horne's generous friendship for America. There is in this book a fine steel engraving of Horne, which gives you the impression that he was a man of refinement, intelligence, and of solid character, Our venerable friend, Hon. Benjamin D. Silliman, of Brooklyn, tells me he remembers Mr. Graham very well. Lord Campbell, in referring to the trial, speaks of Horne's "great acuteness and power of sarcasm." In *Table Talks*, by Samuel Rogers, several instances are given of Horne's wit and repartee.

This seeming diversion is made that it might more clearly appear what manner of man Mansfield had to deal with, at the interesting trial when Horne was a defendant charged with a vile libel on the Government. Mansfield for many years had been a powerful Tory in British politics. That he was, all his public life, a man of great ability and learning, especially in jurisprudence, and much respected, is not questioned. His decision in the famous Somerset (slave) case in 1771, in favor of liberty, will be remembered. This is Lord Campbell's estimate of Mansfield as Chief Justice :

"I think it must be admitted that he is one of the greatest who has ever appeared, and that while he impartially dealt out justice to the litigants who appeared before him, by the enlightened principles which he laid down and the wise rules which he established, he materially improved the jurisprudence of his country. This is surely fame little inferior to that of winning battles or making discoveries in science."

While in a court room, Daniel Webster wrote a letter to his friend, Mr. Blatchford, in 1849, saying :

"Mr. B. R. Curtis is now replying to Mr. Choate on a

law question. He is very clear, and has competent learning. His great mental characteristic is clearness, and the power of clear statement is the great power at the bar. Chief Justice Marshall possessed it in a most remarkable degree, so does Lord Lyndhurst. If to this character of clearness you add fullness and force, you make a man, whether as a lawyer, an historian, or indeed poet, whose discourse or writing merits application of those lines of Sir John Denham's " *Cooper's Hill :* "

> "Though deep, yet clear; though gentle, yet not dull;
> Strong, without rage; without o'erflowing, full."

Mr. Webster adds : "I think the judgment of Lord Mansfield came the nearest to this high standard."

When the troubles of his government with the American Colonies began to be serious, there was no public functionary in Great Britain more ready to serve George the Third, or more certain of the speedy triumph of the Crown over the Colonies, than Lord Mansfield. Mansfield's prolonged and bitter controversies with Chatham, who tried in befriending America to serve his own country the better, give abundant evidence of his intense partisanship for the Crown in the struggle of the Colonies. Mansfield advocated the Stamp Act and aided in preparing it, and refused to listen to arguments for its repeal until, as he said, the Americans were first compelled to submit to the power of Parliament, and exhibit "the most entire obedience before an inquiry could be had into their grievances." These and similar opinions made the Chief Justice a target for Junius, as his unmerciful attacks upon Mansfield show.

British arrogance was shown in many ways, more before the surrender of Burgoyne than in the later years of the war, an instance of which was exhibited by Lord Stormont, whom Franklin and his associate, Mr. Dean, had addressed twice by letter in 1777 as to the cruel treatment of American prisoners, and proposals for exchange. The first letter of February 23d was not noticed by Stormont, but after another, of April 2d, was sent, his lordship wrote an insolent reply, saying : "The King's ambassador receives no applications from rebels, unless they come to implore his Majesty's mercy." Franklin and Dean sent the letter back, saying : "In answer to a letter which concerns some of the most material interests of humanity and of the two nations, Great Britain and the United States of America, now at war, we received the enclosed indecent paper as coming from your Lordship, which we return for your Lordship's more mature consideration." This correspondence is given by Bigelow in his life and letters of Franklin. But in April, 1778, after Burgoyne's surrender, we find the tone changed, and overtures made to Franklin at Paris as to terms of peace. All this change from arrogance to anxiety came too late to help Mr. Horne. Enough has been said to show by what animus Mansfield was moved in the trial of Horne. Though the Colonies had many friends in England the war against them was popular there, and Mansfield's herculean efforts to crush the rebellion and maintain British ascendancy were generally approved. The prosecuting officer at the trial was Lord Thurlow, then the Attorney-General. Extended reference to the distinguished career of Lord Thurlow need not here be made. It is sufficient to say that in vigorously conducting the trial for the Government he was full of enthusiastic and savage loyalty to the King, and held the American Colonies in the usual Tory contempt.

Here, then, we have a group of distinguished and eminent men taking part or coming into notice in this trial. There was Lord Mansfield, presiding, and his associate, Lord Aston, and Lord Thurlow prosecuting, as Attorney-General, aided by two able London lawyers. The defendant was a man of remarkable qualities, as we have seen. Then Dr. Franklin comes into notice as the proposed almoner of the fund raised by subscription for the Lexington sufferers. The battle of Lexington occurred about two weeks before Dr. Franklin's arrival back in America from London, where he had been in service as a representative of American interests, and especially as an agent of the Province of Massachusetts Bay. As all Europe knew, Franklin was a master mind in American affairs. Before this legal tribunal were the great questions involved in the Declaration of Independence. It is not easy to find in legal history, a trial conducted by such eminent jurists and involving questions of such national importance. As the trial proceeded, the mighty power of British public opinion, supporting an arrogant King, was felt there and elsewhere. With such gigantic forces against him, poor Mr. Horne had an unequal contest and a hard time. Few felt or dared to express sympathy for him. In short, Britain gave him the " marble heart."

The trial is reported in about thirty folio pages of the eleventh volume of *"A Complete Collection of State Trials and Proceedings for High Treason and Other Offences,"* commencing with the 11th year of the reign of King Richard the Second, and ending with the 16th year of the reign of King George the Third, published in London in 1781. The proceedings were published by the defendant, Mr. Horne, from Gurney's shorthand notes. The first part of the trial, up to and including the verdict, was before a jury and Lord Mansfield as Chief Justice, and his associate, Aston, of King's Bench, at Guildhall. The second part of the trial, including argument on motion for judgment, was in the Court of King's Bench, Westminster. The trial before the jury began, as it happened, on our Independence Day, July 4th, and the later proceedings were on the 19th and 24th of November, 1777. The charge against the defendant, stated in plain terms, was that at a special meeting of the Constitutional Society, the defendant, Horne, at King's Arms Tavern, Cornhill, June 7th, 1775, during an adjournment of said Society, proposed that a subscription should be immediately entered into by such of the members present who might approve the purpose, for raising the sum of 100 pounds. to be applied to the relief of the widows, orphans and aged parents of our beloved American fellow subjects, who, faithful to the character of Englishmen, preferring death to slavery, were, for that reason only, inhumanly murdered by the King's troops at or near Lexington and Concord, in the province of Massachusetts, on the 19th day of April, 1775. It was further alleged that the sum was immediately collected, and it was thereupon resolved that Mr. Horne do pay the next day into the hands of Messrs. Brownes & Collinson, the said sum of 100 pounds, and that Dr. Franklin be requested to apply the same to the above mentioned purpose. Further technical allegations of the information of the Attorney-General were " that the said John Horne, in contempt of our said Lord and King, and in open violation of the laws of this kingdom, to the evil and pernicious example of all others in the like case offending, and also against the peace of our said present Sovereign Lord, the King, his Crown and dignity, did these things, and the said Attorney-General of our said Lord, the King, further gives the Court here to understand and be informed that said John Horne, being such person as aforesaid, again unlawfully, wickedly, maliciously and seditiously, intending, devising and contriving, as aforesaid, afterwards, to wit : on the 9th day of June, in the fifteenth year aforesaid, with force and arms, at London aforesaid, in the parish and ward aforesaid, wickedly, maliciously and seditiously printed and published, and caused and procured to be printed and published in a certain newspaper, entitled ' *The Morning Chronicle, and London Advertiser,*' a certain other false, wicked, malicious, scandalous and seditious libel of and concerning his said Majesty's government and the employment of his troops, according to the tenor and effect following, that is to say." The substance of the former allegation is here repeated, with the additional statement of the publication, and the newspaper's name. The form of the accusation was that of information in the King's Bench, by the Attorney-General, for libel. This proceeding is reached in our modern practice, in result, by indictment before a grand jury. The law of England permitted the Attorney-General to proceed by information, and not by indictment, if he so determined. The information goes on to allege the payment of the money raised to Dr. Franklin, for the purposes stated, and is signed by E. Thurlow, the Attorney-General.

There seems to have been no difficulty in procuring a jury, and the proceedings opened by a long argument *pro* and *con*, on the question of the right of the Attorney-General to reply to the defendant's argument. This discussion, though extended, is not important for the purposes of this paper. Lord Mansfield ruled that the Attorney-General could reply if he saw cause to do so. Near the close of the argument Lord Mansfield seems to have lost his patience, and said to Horne: "There must be an end." Mr. Horne replied: "Not of this objection?" Lord Mansfield said: "No, but an end of going out of the case. You must behave decently and properly." Mr. Horne replied: "I will surely behave properly." Then Mr. Horne, who seems to have been fond of satire, said: "Now, then, my Lord, I entreat you to let me 'decently' tell you of the situation you have put me into." The witnesses examined for the Government proved the handwriting of the alleged libeller to be that of Mr. Horne, and also the publication of the newspapers by the printers, and then the Attorney-General rested. Mr. Horne was careful to prove, on cross-examination of one of the printers, that he told this printer that he asked no favors, and, if the Government intervened, to disclose at once who was the author of the circular and advertisement. The Attorney-General then rested his case, saying: "My Lord, we have done." Mr. Horne then proceeded to address the jury, and in his first sentence hit the judge, saying: "I am much happier, gentlemen, in addressing myself to you, and believe I shall be much more fortunate, as well as happy, than in addressing myself to the judge." Abruptness between the bench and the bar seems to have been the style of that period, another instance of which was, when Dunning—afterwards Lord Ashburton—was stating the law to a jury at Guildhall, Lord Mansfield interrupted him, saying: "If that be law, I'll go home and burn my books." "My Lord," replied Dunning, "you had better go home and read them." Horne reminds the jury that the verdict must be their own, and not the judge's. He complains that the proceedings against him are by information of the Attorney-General *ex-officio*. He says, that by information the Attorney-General may accuse whom he pleases, and what he pleases, and when he pleases, and all this without resort to a grand jury, and that because it is the pretended suit of the crown. He urged that he ought not to be accused on the *ipse dixit* of the Attorney-General, but upon the oaths of witnesses that are called before a grand jury upon their responsibility when they find an indictment. It seems that at this moment the notorious Mr. Wilkes was sitting near Lord Mansfield on the bench, and having some pleasant conversation, accompanied by smiles, though in former years Mansfield and Wilkes had been intensely antagonistic. Horne mentions that they are both laughing, he supposes, at his expense. He declares

16

that he will say "murder" again and again, when troops kill people unlawfully. He says that if there was no war in America, when the people at Lexington were killed, then it is right to call it "murder," and urges that it could not be said there was a war until after General Gage issued his proclamation of warning, which was after the battle of Lexington. Before that, *America* did not know it; how, then, could he, Mr. Horne, be expected to know it?

Horne said to the jury: "Gentlemen, I shall desire, by-and-by, for your satisfaction and mine, to find out whether there is one man in the country that believes me guilty of the crime laid to my charge; a crime that is to have a punishment which is called by the law a temporary death, and exclusion from society, imprisonment." He charged that the apparent object of this prosecution is "to take what little money out of my pocket I may have there, and to imprison me and exclude me from that society of which I have rendered myself unworthy." It gives him pleasure, he says, " to see that there is " (referring to Wilkes) "by the judge who is now trying me, a gentleman who, as well as myself, has charged the King's troops with murder; a charge which, at that time, excited great abhorrence and detestation against him. The judge and that gentleman have enjoyed each other's company exceedingly." This remark caused laughter in the audience. "Well, gentlemen," turning towards Lord Mansfield and Mr. Wilkes, "I have caused another laugh between the gentlemen. It gives me pleasure to think, if I am to come out of prison—if you are so kind as to put me there—I, too, may have the honor, if it be one, of sitting cheek by cheek with the judge, and laughing at some other libeller." In the course of his four hours' argument Mr. Horne declares this oppressive prosecution against him by the Attorney-General, who is the tool of the Minister, is not for crimes against the constitution, but for partial political opinions, and they who are pil-loried or imprisoned to-day may be, for the same act, pensioned to-morrow, just as the hands change; if this party goes down, it is libel; if it comes up, it is merit. He asserts that it was true, that under a good Minister there are no prosecutions for libel; under a bad Minister, you meet with little else. He takes the ground that what might be a libel if written now, may not have been a libel at the time it was written; in other words, his view was that when he published his advertisement in the newspapers, it was not really understood that there was a war in America; but now that the war has been going on for two years, if a similar publication were made it would be more open to the charge of libel on the King and Government. It seems that the Government had previously put the printers on trial, where there was a conviction and a sentence, but the sentence was suspended, and referring to this, he says: "If they justify their sentence on the printers, I will justify the Court for the most ample punishment they can inflict on me. If I am guilty, no man on earth so guilty; it was the most deliberate act of my life; it was thought of long before I did it. I made the motion ; I caused the meeting ; I subscribed a great part of the money ; I procured the rest from my particular intimate friends." He argues that the work of the Attorney-General, in pushing the prosecution, is not creditable to him or his Government, and that what occurred at the so-called battle of Lexington was, in fact, murder. He then reads in evidence, a report of the battle, by an officer in the British army, who took part in it, one Captain Edward Thoroton Gould. I do not remember to have seen this report of the battle in any American book, and, as it is short and easily understood, will read it.

"I, Edward Thoroton Gould, of His Majesty's Own regiment of foot, being of lawful age, do testify and declare, that on the evening of the 18th instant, under the orders of General Gage, I embarked with the light infantry and grenadiers of the line, commanded by Colonel Smith, and landed on the marshes of Cambridge, from whence we proceeded to Lexington. On our arrival at the place, we saw a body of provincial troops, armed, to the number of sixty or seventy men. On our approach, they dispersed, and soon after firing began; but which party fired first I cannot exactly say, as our troops rushed on, shouting and huzzaing previous to the firing, which was continued by our troops so long as any of the provincials were to be seen. From thence we marched to Concord. On a hill near the entrance of the town we saw another body of the provincials assembled. Six companies of light infantry were ordered down to take possession of the bridge, which the provincials retreated over. The company I commanded was one. Three companies of the above detachment went forward about two miles. In the meantime the provincial troops returned to the number of about three or four hundred. We drew up on the Concord side of the bridge. The provincials came down upon us, upon which we engaged and gave the first fire. This was the first engagement after the one at Lexington. A continued fire from both parties lasted through the whole day. I, myself, was wounded at the attack of the bridge, and am now treated with the greatest humanity and taken all possible care of by the provincials at Medford.

(Signed)   EDWARD THOROTON GOULD."

It will be seen, in all Horne's contention, that upon this statement of the battle of Lexington, by a British officer, that it appears that the British were the aggressors; that they fired upon the people without any justifiable provocation, and what the British troops did, therefore, in killing, was, in fact, murder. In this connection it may be stated, as a justification of this view, to some extent, that not only had the press of America declared it to be murder, but some of the London papers were saying so, so that if Horne fell into a legal error in thus characterizing the battle, he had considerable authority for his view. Horne says that he bases his action upon principle; he says he has accused the Government "because I thought it my duty; my motive has been constantly the same; I know no America." He quotes Solon as saying, when asked which was the best government, "Where those who are not personally injured resent and pursue the injury or violence done to another as he would if done to himself. That," said Horne, "was the best kind of government, and Solon had a law passed empowering men to do so. By our laws, the whole of the neighborhood is answerable for the conduct of each. Our laws make it each man's duty and interest to watch over the conduct of all. .This principle and motive has been represented in me as malice. It is the only malice they will ever find about me. They have, in no part of my life, found me in any court of justice upon any personal contest or motive whatever, either for interest, or profit, or injury." Horne then denied that he had charged the King's troops with murder. The point was that he had intended to so charge the King's government.

Referring to Lexington, Franklin also speaks of "murder" in a letter to his friend, Wm. Strahan, dated at Philadelphia, July 5th, 1775, saying: "You are a member of Parliament, and one of that majority which has doomed my country to destruction. You begun to burn our towns and murder our people. Look upon your hands; they are stained with the blood of your relatives. You and I were long friends; you are now my enemy, and I am yours." On the question of "murder," Horne continues: "And now, gentlemen, picture to yourself the Americans of Lexington and Concord, sleeping quietly in their beds, their wives and their infants by their sides, roused at the dead of night with an alarm that a numerous body of the King's troops (their numbers, perhaps, augmented by fear and report), were marching toward them, by surprise, in a hostile manner. These troops, who might not be brought to justice by them for any murders which they might commit. What shall they do? Shall they take to flight, and leave the helpless part of their family behind them, or shall they stay and submit themselves and their families to the licentiousness of these ruffians? I suppose there might be among them (as among us) some of both these sorts; it is, however, for the honor of human nature, that there were also some of another temper, and they hastily armed themselves as well as they could. There is nothing surely in this that will justify the slaughter of them which ensued. You will please to observe the time when this happened, for it is a very striking fact. As soon as the Act of Parliament, exempting them from the trial for murder in America, got to America, and the weather would permit them, the troops did instantly, without delay, do these murders with which I now charge them. That Act of Parliament was proposed by the confidential friend of my judge, Lord George Germaine, and the Attorney and Solicitor-General were instructed to bring in the Bill he proposed in the Committee. The General of the army was at that time the Civil Governor of the town." Horne said that the charge that the King's troops committed murder was published in the London news-papers of May 30th and 31st, 1775, and he believed it to be true. The charge was supported by affidavits taken on the spot and lodged with the Lord Mayor of London, and signed by Mr. Arthur Lee. I have read enough, perhaps, to indicate the tone and general idea of Horne's defence. As Horne had apparently concluded, the Attorney-General began to address the jury in reply, when Horne rose and addressed Lord Mansfield, saying that he was ashamed to say that he had forgotten to examine some witnesses, but hoped the Attorney-General would consent that he might now do so. The Attorney-General replying that he should "object, except he should open to what points he meant to call them." Lord Mansfield replied: "You had better not object, Mr. Attorney-General, you had better hear his witnesses." And it was so ordered. "Call your witnesses," said the Court. "I call the Attorney-General," said Horne. "Oh, you cannot examine the Attorney-General," said Mansfield. "Does your Lordship so deliver that as the law? My Lord, I call the Attorney-General and desire that the book may be given to him." An extended colloquy went on, and Lord Mansfield ruled that he could not force the Attorney-General to be examined. Then Horne called Lord George Germaine, and it was said that he had gone to Germany. "Yes," said Horne, "he has gone to Germany, too, I suppose, with General Gage." Then Mr. Alderman Oliver was called and sworn as a witness. His testimony related to what took place in the Constitutional Society, as to raising the 100 pounds and publishing the advertisement. Sir Theodore Stephen Jannsen, a subscriber to the fund, was called, and proved nothing but what Horne had already admitted to be true. A Mr. Wm. Lacey was called, who proved that the 100 pounds was duly paid over to be used by Dr. Franklin, and the receipt of the bankers was produced.

Mr. Edward Thoroton Gould was sworn, and he gave some account of the battle, the substance of which is embodied in his report. One curious question is asked of Gould. "Pray, do you know that the Americans, upon that occasion, scalped any of our troops?" Answer: "I heard they did it; I did not see them." Question: "From whom did you hear it ?" Answer: "From a Captain that advanced up the country." Horne asked officer Gould: "Did you know, had you any intelligence that the Americans of Lexington and Concord were at that time marching, or intending to march, to attack you at Boston ?" Answer: "We supposed that they were marching to attack us from continued firing of alarm guns, cannon, as they appeared to be such from the reports." Lord Mansfield: "Cannon?" Answer: "Cannon." Question: "When was that ?" Answer: "As soon as we begun the march, early in the morning." In charging the jury, Lord Mansfield emphasized the fact, that "cannon" were used by the provincials, thus confirming the idea of intended war and justification of the British shooting, which view did not please Horne. After some further questions to Officer Gould, Horne announced that he was through, and rested his case. Then came the address of the Attorney-General to the jury, fiercely urging a conviction. What the Attorney-General's contention was, need not be related at length. It is obvious that it would be, as it was, an able, eloquent, and earnest assault upon Mr. Horne, for libeling the King and the Government, in proposing that the fund should be applied to the relief of the widows, orphans, and aged parents of "our beloved American fellow-subjects," who, faithful to the character of Englishmen, preferring death to slavery, were, for that reason only, inhumanly murdered by the King's troops, at or near Lexington and Concord, in the Province of Massachusetts. The Attorney-General exclaims: "What does that evidence amount to ? Why, that the King's troops, under the command of General Gage, were in a hostile country, and that it was impossible for them to go upon any service, ordered by their general and conducted by his officers, without an attack; that the moment they went out of Boston alarm guns were discharged, in order to rouse the power that possessed the country, and to make the attack upon them, and this is the medium by which it is to be proved, that the soldiers who were ordered by their commander to advance from their post at Boston into that country, were guilty of murder, because they were surrounded, upon the 18th and 19th of April, in consequence of those alarm guns, with an armed force on the other side, in order to withstand and oppose their operations, they being at that time in a hostile country. Why, if I had meant, if I had thought it consistent with law or with reason, to enter into a discussion of that question with him, whether he is a libeller or not, for having charged them with murder, by a printed paper, instead of charging them in a more direct way; if I had thought it necessary to establish the case against him in the strongest and most precise manner, it would have been by calling just such a witness as that, in order to prove that the troops were themselves attacked, and that upon the moment of their going out of the place, they were surrounded by hostile people. But, 'necessity,' it seems—necessity, according to Horne's notion of the law—is that which his defense prescribes; that a man must go to the wall who is attacked; he must fly first, and, if he can escape by flight, then he shall not justify himself by turning and repelling the attack. That the King's troops, when they heard the alarm guns and were attacked, were to fly, to get to the wall and drop their arms. This is the notion of military disposition in a hostile country, and this is the law that the learned gentleman has learned from the state trials, the source of his reading, and which he has set forth with a dexterity and a species of understanding which is peculiar to him."

Again, the Attorney-General says "that no one doubts but that the intention constitutes the criminality of every charge of every denomination and kind; but the extreme ridicule of the thing is in his talking of that doctrine upon an information like this. See what it is : The words are, 'that the American subjects, for meritorious considerations upon their part, and for those considerations only, were inhumanly murdered at Lexington and Concord, in the province of Massachusetts Bay.' Nobody can doubt in the world, but that imputing inhuman murder to the attack of those troops is abuse. I suppose he did not mean it as flattery, to extol them, to deliver them down to posterity (if such paragraphs as these have any chance of reaching down to posterity) in terms of heroism. He meant to abuse. The words themselves are abuse, and then, I say, when words of direct, unqualified, indubitable abuse are printed concerning any man alive, the very circumstances of printing calumny concerning a man, carries along with it an intention to abuse him.   Why, it is nonsense to doubt it. One may spin words till one loses the meaning of a sentence and the first words that are used in the sentence, but it is nonsense to deny when you use direct abuse; when you revile them in the very attempt to justify the charge and again use terms of abuse, that those terms of abuse do not prove intention of abuse; *prima facie* at least they will."

And so the Attorney's address went on, based, of course, upon the assumption that the people of America were vile rebels who were taking up arms against the British Government without just cause, and that it was a terrible offence for the defendant to commit, to uphold these men after they began to perpetrate their offences of disorder and open rebellion, as they did from the British standpoint at Lexington and Concord.   Finding Horne a man of considerable attainments, and not a little influence, using the press in favor of the provincials, and raising money to support their widows and orphans and aged parents, and accusing the Government and the King's troops of murder in the battle of Lexington, there was nothing left, said the Attorney-General, to do, but to bring on this prosecution that such an offence as Horne's might be duly punished.

When Lord Mansfield came to charge the jury, he said the question was : "Did Horne compose and publish—that is, was he the author and publisher of it ?"   As to that, he said, there can be no question, as the proof was clear, and Horne did not deny it.   He then said: "there remains nothing more but that which reading the paper must enable you to form an opinion on, superior to all arguments in the world, and this is the sense of the paper, that arraignment of the Government and the employment of the troops upon the occasion of Lexington mentioned in that paper.   Read it.   You will form the conclusion yourselves.   What is it ?   Why it is this: that our beloved American fellow-subjects (therefore innocent men) in rebellion against the State—they are our fellow-subjects—but not so absolutely beloved without exception.   Beloved to many purposes; beloved to be reclaimed; beloved to be forgiven; beloved to have good done to them, but not beloved so as to be abetted in their rebellion. And there-fore that certainly conveys the idea that they are innocent. But, further, it says that they were inhumanly murdered at Lexington by the King's troops, merely on account of their acting like Englishmen and preferring liberty to slavery."

Again, he says: "The unhappy resistance of the legis-lative authority of this kingdom by many of our fellow-subjects in America, is too calamitous an event not to be impressed upon all your minds; all the steps leading to it are of the most universal notoriety. The legislature of this kingdom have avowed that the Americans rebelled because they wanted to shake off the sovereignty of this kingdom. They profess only to bring them back to be subjects, and to quell rebellion. Troops are employed, money is expended upon this ground ; that the case is here between a just government and rebellious subjects, for a just and good purpose, for the benefit of the whole. If I do not mistake, the first hostilities that were com-mitted, (though many steps leading to them existed before), were those upon the 19th of April, 1775. If some soldiers, without authority, had got into a drunken fray. and murder had ensued, and this paper could relate to that, it would be quite a different thing from the charge in the information, because it is charged as a seditious libel, tending to disquiet the minds of the people. Now, what evidence has Mr. Gould given ?"

The judge then repeated Officer Gould's statement. In considering this libel, the judge told the jury that they must judge whether it contains a harmless, innocent proposition for the good and welfare of this kingdom, the support of the legislative government, and the King's authority according to law, or, whether it is not denying the Government and legislative authority of England, and justifying the Americans, averring that they are totally innocent, and that they only desire not to be slaves; not disputing to be subjects, but that they desire only not to be slaves. and that the use that is made of the King's troops upon this occasion was to reduce them to slavery. And if it was intended to convey that meaning, there can be little doubt whether that is an arraingment of the Govern-ment and of the troops employed by them or not. But that is a matter for your judgment. You will judge of the meaning of it. You will judge of the subject to which it applied and connect them together, and, if it is a criminal arraignment of these troops acting under the orders of the officers employed by the Government of this country to charge them with murder of innocent subjects, because they would not be slaves, you will find your verdict but one way ; but, if you are of the opinion that the contest is to reduce innocent subjects to slavery, and that they were all murdered (like the cases of the noted murders of Glencoe, and twenty other massacres that might be named), why, then you will form a different conclusion, with regard to the meaning and application of this paper. I pass over a great deal that was said, because it ought not to have been said."

The jury withdrew about five o'clock, and returned into court about half an hour after six ; and gave in their verdict that the defendant was guilty. The court was then adjourned to Wednesday, November 19th, 1777, when the Attorney-General moved for judgment against Mr. Horne. The information was then read by order of the court. Mr. Horne then made an extended argument for arrest of judgment, in which he repeated much that he had said to the jury. The Attorney-General then made a vigorous reply and Horne answered him. Among other things, Horne claimed that there was not sufficient averment in the information that there was a rebellion in Massachusetts Bay, and that certain persons were employed to quell that rebellion. If the information had averred it, it would have been necessary to prove it, and it could not have been proved as an existing fact on the 19th day of April, 1775. Horne went into a critical discussion of his proposition, which seemed to trouble Lord Mansfield considerably. Finally, Lord Mansfield said : "Mr. Attorney-General, have you anything to say ? " The Attorney-General said: " It belongs to the defendant, I apprehend, to state what he can in his extenuation." Then Mr. Horne said: "I shall state nothing in extenuation until your Lordship's decision has told me that there was a crime. I do not know where the crime lies at present. My objection goes that there is no crime averred in the information. It is impossible for me to extenuate that which I do not acknowledge." Lord Mansfield: "Have you any affidavits of the circumstances, or anything?" Mr. Horne: "None in the world." Lord Mansfield: "Let him be committed." Mr. Horne: "Will your Lordship commit me before it appears whether I am even accused of any crime?" Lord Mansfield: "No. Then you may come up on Monday. You came voluntarily now?" Mr. Horne: "I did." Lord Mansfield: "Then come up voluntarily again. If you should find any precedents on either side, I wish you would give them to us." This was repeated to both the Attorney-General and Horne two or three times. Horne replied that he was not himself very likely to produce precedents.

When the court again convened on November 24th, 1777, Lord Mansfield read an elaborate opinion on the point raised by Horne as to the sufficiency of the information. The decision was that the information was sufficient. Perhaps Horne, upon hearing the judge's decision, felt as did the late Hon. Joseph Payne, of the Boston bar, who, when learnedly arguing a law question before a Supreme Court judge in Boston, was interrupted by the judge, who said: "Mr. Payne, that is not law." "I know it," said Payne, "but it was before your Honor spoke." I am inclined to believe that our Bar and our Courts would be of the opinion that the missing averment was essential, and that Horne was right.

In deciding the motion for arrest of judgment, Lord Mansfield read Captain Gould's report of the battle, and said :

"Defendant alleges that the charge, as it stands upon the record, is insufficient in law to support any judgment; that there was no averment as to the state of the Massachusetts Colony at that time; either that there were riots, insurrections, or rebellion; that there were no averments that the King had sent any troops; that there was no averment that there was any skirmish or engagement, or how it began, or how it went on, or ended; and that it was not averred that the employment of the troops was by the King's authority. The only objection that had color in it was, what I mentioned last, that the employment of the troops was not averred to be by the King's authority. I thought then, and said, that ·the averment of the words being written 'of and concerning the King's Government' was an answer, but no precedent was cited or alluded to on either side. I fancy the Attorney-General was surprised with the objection. But there was no precedent, and I could not say upon my memory whether precedents might not require some technical form of expression as to that medium through which words are averred to be written of the King's Government. And if any flaw had happened, technically or verbally, that were not at all founded in the sense or reason of the thing, I should, in this case, be of the same opinion that I was in the case of an outlawry, that the defendant ought to have the benefit of it. And therefore, I desired that we might think of it for some time, that precedents might be searched, and the books looked into. We have fully considered of it, and the precedents have been looked into, and we have fully considered the information and all the objections that were mentioned, and all the objections that we could think of; and we are all clearly of opinion, without any doubt, that the information is sufficient. An indictment or information must charge what, in law, constitutes the crime, with such certainty as must be proved, but that certainty may arise from necessary inference, in the manner settled in the case of the King and Lawley, in Strange. Plain words in a libel speak for themselves. If they are doubtful, their meaning must be ascertained by an inuendo. Here the words are plain, they want no inuendo. They are averred to be written 'of and concerning the King's Government and the employment of his troops.' The obvious meaning is, that the employment of the King's troops must be under his authority, and it necessarily is so, if the words relate to and are written of and concerning the King's Government. This must now be taken to be true, because the verdict finds it. Had the question arisen upon a demurrer, it must equally have been taken to be true. The gist of every charge of every libel consists in the person or matter of and concerning whom or which the words are averred to be said or written. In the King against Alderton the information was held bad, because it was not laid in the information; it was not laid that the libel was of or concerning the justices of Suffolk.

Where the words are averred to be written of the King's Government, (there are several precedents), or of the government of the kingdom, or of the government, suppose, of the navy, as to anything further as to which they are also written through the medium of which they calumniate the King's Government, there is no form of expression technically necessary. And it cannot be, because there may be cases where the King's Government might be calumniated through an imputation upon the gross licentiousness of the King's troops. The question to be tried is, whether the words laid are written of the King's Government. It may vary the degree of mischief, guilt or malice, but it is immaterial as to the constitution of the crime upon the record, whether the words refer to something that has existed or are an entire fiction. Had Lexington been left out, or had any other place been mentioned, where there had been no skirmishes or engagement, instead of Lexington, it would, without any inuendo, have been equally a libel. It is the duty of the jury to construe plain words and clear allusions to matters of universal notoriety, according to their obvious meaning, and as everybody else who reads must under-stand them. But the defendant may give evidence to show that, in the case in question, they were used in a different or in a qualified sense. If no such evidence is given, the obvious meaning to every man's understanding must be decisive. Before this trial five several juries had found those words, from their necessary meaning, to be of and concerning the King's Government. Here, in this case, the defendant gave evidence, and the evidence he gave demonstrated that the words related to *troops acting under the King's authority*, and consequently related to the King's Government. And I am more confirmed that upon this occasion there is *little color of doubt of any flaw* in the information, that in those five trials that I allude to, in one or other of them, *a great variety of counsel of learn-ing, eminence and ability* were employed. *They were called upon to pry*, with all the sharpness that they had, into the information, to put holes in it; there were three judgments given upon conviction upon them, and *no counsel saw or imagined there was any flaw in it*. Therefore we are all satisfied that the information is sufficient."

The Attorney-General then addressed the Court, saying, among other things, that Horne had charged that the national force of this country has been employed in the murder of the King's subjects, for as meritorious an attribute as may be imputed to man, and he has specified the time and place at which that was done. He then proceeded to characterize the libel in very severe terms. The Attorney-General said he believed it would be "totally impossible for the imagination of any man, however shrewd, to state a libel more scandalous and base than in the fact imputed; more malignant and hostile to the country in which the libeller was born; more dangerous in example, if it was suffered to pass unpunished, than this which I have now stated to your Lordship. It was impossible," he said, "by any epithets to aggravate it." He then reflected upon the conduct of the defendant, in seeming to glorify himself for his conduct, as if adding crime to crime, and showed himself to be defiant of justice. The Attorney-General then referred to his duty to submit to the Court his views, as to what the punishment should be. He said that "the punishments to be inflicted for misdemeanors of this sort have usually been of three different kinds : fine, corporal punishment by imprisonment, and infamy, by the judgment of the pillory. With regard to the fine, it is impossible for justice to make this sort of punishment however the infamy will, always fall upon the offender: because it is well known that men who have more wealth, who have better and more respectful situations and reputations to be watched over, employ men in desperate situations, both of circumstances and character, in order to do that which serves their party purposes; and when the punishment comes to be inflicted, this Court must have regard to the apparent situation and the circumstances of the man employed; that is, of the man convicted, with regard to the punishment. With regard to imprisonment, that is a species of punishment not to be considered alike in all cases, but varies with the person who is to be the object of it, and so varies with the person that it would be proper for the judgment of the court to state circumstances which will make the imprisonment fall lighter or heavier, as the truth is upon the person presented to the

Court. The defendant has asserted that imprisonment was no kind of inconvenience to him; that it was a mere matter of circumstances whether it happened in one place or another, and that the longest imprisonment which this Court could inflict for punishment was not beyond the reach of accommodation. In this respect, therefore, imprisonment is not only, as with respect to the person, not an adequate punishment to the offence, but, the public are told, and told by a pamphlet which bears the reverend gentleman's name, (may be his name may have been forged to it), that it would be no punishment. I stated, in the third place, to your Lordship, the pillory to have been the usual punishment for this species of offence."

The Attorney-General then went on to urge that the defendant should be punished by the judgment of the pillory.

Mr. Horne again addressed the Court, repeating some things that he had said before, and, among other things, said: "My Lords, the Attorney-General has attempted to alarm me with monstrous fines, long imprisonments, with infamous punishment. My Lords, infamy is as little acquainted with my name as with that of the gentleman's, or with your Lordships. I feel no apprehension from the pillory. I do feel some little pain, that a gentleman, taking advantage, should say and offer those things, unfounded in the appearance even of truth against me, which neither he, nor any other man like him, dare to insinuate in any other station but this. My Lords, I never in my life solicited a favor; I never desired to meet with compassion." He further said: "My Lords, Mr. Attorney-General has said that I represented imprisonment as no kind of inconvenience. As no kind of inconvenience, my Lords, will not certainly be true, because the great luxury of my life is a very small, but a very clean, cottage; and, though imprisonment will be so far inconvenient to me, the cause of it will make it not painful." Again, he says: "My Lords, Mr. Attorney-General has done what I had before heard attempted to be done, with very great sorrow; he has attempted to re-instate the Star Chamber. The fault he finds with it is only its rankness—before the prosecutions grew so rank in the Star Chamber (and which rankness caused it to be abolished). I do not recollect the words of that act by which it was abolished, but, I am sure that its rankness alone is not the reason given. If that gentleman would lend me his memory, I should then repeat that none of the powers, nor none like them (your Lordships will know better the words) ever to be put in use again in that or any other court." He closed by saying: "There are many other things which I might say to your Lordships; but, as I trust, and fully trust, that I shall still find a remedy, my Lords, against the present decision, I shall forbear saying one syllable in extenuation of what the Attorney-General has been pleased to charge me with, and leave your Lordships to pronounce your judgment, without the least consideration of me; without the smallest desire, too, that you should abate a hair from what you think necessary for the justice of my country. I shall leave it entirely to your Lordships' discretion."

Then Mr. Justice Aston, sitting with Lord Mansfield, opened the vials of his British wrath upon sentencing Horne, as follows:

"John Horne, Clerk, you stand convicted upon an information filed against you by his Majesty's Attorney-General, of writing and publishing, and causing to be written and published, a false, wicked and seditious libel, of and concerning his Majesty's Government and the employment of his troops. The record has been openly read in court from the record;" and then, in referring to the terms of the same, the Court said:

"Upon that the Court has now decided agreeably to the finding of the jury, and no man can really mistake the malicious meaning and insinuation of it; it is a libel which contains a most audacious insult upon his Majesty's administration and Government, and the conduct of his loyal troops employed in America. It treats those disaffected and traitorous persons who have been in arms in open rebellion against his Majesty, as faithful subjects; faithful to the character of Englishmen, and it falsely and seditiously asserts that for that reason only, they were inhumanly murdered by his Majesty's troops at Lexington and Concord. By this same libel, subscriptions, too, are proposed and promoted for the families of those very rebels who fell in that cause, traitorously fighting against the troops of their lawful sovereign. This is the light in which this libel must appear to every man of sound and impartial understanding; this is the plain and unartificial sense of it; the contents of this libel have been too effectually scattered and dispersed by your means, as charged, and they have been inserted in divers and different newspapers; the contents are too well known—I trust, abhorred —to need any repetition from me for the sake of observing further upon their malice, sedition and falsity. The Court hath considered of the punishment fit to be inflicted upon you for this offence, and the sentence of the Court is, that you do pay a fine to the King of 200 pounds; that you be imprisoned for the space of twelve months, and until that fine be paid, and that upon the determination of your imprisonment, you do find sureties for your good behaviour for three years, yourself in 400 pounds, and two sureties in 200 pounds each."

Mr. Horne : "My Lords, I am not at all aware of what is meant by finding sureties for good behaviour for three years. It is that part of the sentence that, perhaps, I shall find the most difficulty to comply with, because I do not understand it. If I am not irregular in entreating your Lordship to explain it to me; your Lordship, I suppose, would choose to have your sentences plainly understood, as I know not the nature of this suretyship."

Lord Mansfield said : "It is a common addition."
Mr. Horne said: "And it may be a common hardship."
Mr. Justice Aston: "Not to repeat offences of this sort."
Lord Mansfield : "Any misdemeanor." Mr. Justice Aston: "Whatever shall be considered bad behaviour."
Mr. Horne: "If your Lordship will imprison me for these three years, I should be safer, because I cannot foresee but that the most meritorious action of my life may be considered to be of the same sort." Lord Mansfield: "You must be tried by a jury of your country and be convicted. You know it is a most constant addition. You know that, yourself, very well. Where are the tipstaves ?" (Which, in modern phrase, would mean: "Officers, take the prisoner in charge.").

Dr. Johnson, inquiring about it, said : "I hope they did not put the dog in the pillory; he has too much literature for that." Boswell says: "Johnson added, 'Were I to make a new edition of my dictionary, I would adopt several of Mr. Horne's etymologies.'"

Lord Campbell, referring to the sentence, remarks: "Thurlow, in a manner which astonishes a modern Attorney-General, pressed that the defendant, who was an ordained clergyman of the Church of England, who was a scholar and a gentleman, should be set in the pillory."

Thurlow, by urging punishment in the pillory, showed an unscrupulous and brutal mind.

In less than a month after Mr. Horne was sent to jail Thurlow was made Lord Chancellor of England, and sat on the woolsack in the House of Lords.

All this shows the fierce resentment aroused by the supporters of the American cause in England.

During his imprisonment he continued his favorite studies, and in 1779 applied for admission to the bar, but was not received, because, as was the rule, he had been a clergyman. He continued active in political discussions for many years, being a candidate for the Commons twice, and defeated, and again a candidate, and elected, in 1801, but the parliament decided not to admit him, ruling that a clergyman could not thereafter sit in the House of Commons.

As another incident in his life it may be stated, that Horne was tried for high treason, mainly for his action as a member of the Constitutional Society, in expressing sympathy for the French Revolution. At this time Horne did not ignore the maxim that "he who acts as his own lawyer has a fool for a client," but was most ably defended by Gibbs, and by the brilliant Lord Erskine, and acquitted.

Six authors have written the life of Horne. Stephens, who wrote Horne's life in 1813, says of him, in reference to the trial for treason: "He conducted himself with great firmness and courage." It was abundantly shown that the charge of treason was trumped up by police spies, who tried to prove that Horne was in a conspiracy to excite a similar revolution in England.

From what has been stated it will be seen what was the temper of the British courts towards the American Revolution. Battles for the King were fought in British forums as well as by British troops in America. British statesmen and courts could not see nor believe that what Chief Justice Mansfield at the trial of Horne referred to as "the occasion at Lexington" portended the independence of the Colonies. Samuel Adams saw it, when he exclaimed: "Oh! what a glorious morning this, for America," as he heard the guns at Lexington. There was a feeling, no doubt, induced somewhat by many assurances from America, that independence was not the object, but rather to procure the repeal of obnoxious statutes and a more conciliatory policy by the home government.

Up to a short time before Lexington, Franklin took this ground, and as late as the 5th of March, 1775, when Dr. Warren delivered the fifth annual oration on the Boston Massacre, in the crowded Old South Church, the orator said that he and his friends "were not seeking independence. But," he added, "there were men in that house who were." In this audience were men of various opinions, including British army officers, who were expected to hear and report. Also, in Parliament, when the trial of Horne and other proceedings were on and before, there was high debate, in which Chatham, and Camden, and North, and Mansfield were engaged, as to what should be the policy in American affairs. That the excitement and trend of public opinion reached the court room can not be doubted. The hope of speedily crushing the Americans, which had animated Lord Mansfield and induced the nation warmly to support the policy of the Government, was cruelly disappointed. Every fresh arrival showed the aspect of affairs to be more and more alarming, and in the course of a few months came the stunning intelligence that General Burgoyne had capitulated at Saratoga. Lord Campbell tells us that when the news of the surrender reached England the poignancy of Mansfield's grief, at seeing all his predictions falsified, was very great.

Horne was a sincere lover of freedom and justice, and naturally opposed the policy of his Government towards the Colonies. When he published his libel, in June 1775, there was little, if any, thought in the British mind of the momentous events that must follow the battle of

Lexington. Hence, the libel seemed most inopportune, unsupported, malicious and absurd. But Horne espoused the American cause because he believed it was right in principle. At the same time it is not necessary to question the sincerity of the British Government in the great controversy. The conviction of Horne may have been correct under British law; he was guilty, perhaps, of a seditious attack on his Government, which was a violation of that law at that time.

When the conflict at Lexington and Concord came there were expanding hopes in the Colonies as to the possible outcome. Paul Revere's spirited ride, upon warning the people, showed the rising spirit of the people, and was a spectacle of heroism and fidelity fitly commemorated in song by Longfellow and others. Here are some of Longfellow's lines :

"In the books you have read,
How the British regulars fired and fled ;
How the farmers gave them ball for ball,
From behind each fence and farm-yard wall.
Chasing the red-coats down the lane,
The crossing the fields to emerge again
Under the trees at the turn of the road,
And only pausing to fire and load.
So, through the night, rode Paul Revere ;
And so, through the night, went back this cry of alarm
To every Middlesex village and farm,
A cry of defiance, and not of fear,
A voice in the darkness, a knock at the door,
And a word that shall echo forevermore."

In less than sixty days Bunker Hill followed. While these and other stirring events were arousing our people, the authorities of Great Britain were taking a different view and were solemnly of the opinion that it was rebellion without justification, and must be put down at every hazard. So when Lord Mansfield made his rulings, and charged the jury in the trial of Horne, he acted, great and able as he was, upon a mistaken view, not perhaps on the technical questions raised, but as to the real meaning of the American uprising. He could not comprehend that the Colonies were to be, "and of right ought to be, free and independent."

In referring to the severe sentence imposed upon Mr. Horne, Lord Brougham said: "Thus a bold and just denunciation of the attack made upon our American brethren, which nowadays would rank among the very mildest and tamest effusions of the periodical press, condemned him to prison for one year." He might have added, "and a loss in fine and costs of 1200 pounds."

Our national Constitution provides that, "Congress shall make no law abridging the freedom of speech, or of the press." Our State Constitutions have similar provisions. We, who are thus protected by such safeguards of freedom, are apt to forget from what darkness we have emerged into the light, and how costly in blood and treasure our progress has been, through inquisitions and massacres. To appreciate this more fully, we must look back, if not further than, to the career of the Twelve English Judges, who under the inspiration of Stuart Kings, crushed freedom of thought and expression in the most tyrannical manner. Here, for instance, is William Pryn, a zealous Puritan and a learned lawyer, who wrote against the corrupt practices in theatres. He was brought to the Star Chamber in 1632, and Chief Justice Richardson, of bad repute, said: "Mr. Pryn, I do declare you to be a schism maker in the church, a sedition sower in the commonwealth, a wolf in sheep's clothing; in a word, *omnium malorum nequissimus*" (the wickedest of all scoundrels). "I shall fine him 10,000 pounds, which is more than he is worth, yet he deserves it. I will not set him at liberty, no more than a mad dog, who though he cannot bite, yet will he foam, he is fit to live in dens with such beasts of prey as wolves and tigers, like himself; therefore, I do condemn him to perpetual imprisonment, as those monsters that are not fit to live among men, nor to see light. I would have him branded in the forehead, slit in the nose, and his ears cropped, too." This part of the sentence was executed the 7th and 10th of May, 1633, thirteen years after the landing of the Pilgrim Fathers. No wonder they left the country.

Now comes the pious and venerable Richard Baxter, selected for a victim, and brought before Judge Jeffreys in the Star Chamber. Baxter's offence was that in a Commentary on the New Testament, he had complained with some bitterness of the persecution which the Dissenters suffered. As Lord Macaulay tells the story, it was adjudged a crime not to use the Prayer Book. For this men had been driven from their homes, stripped of their property, and locked up in dungeons. An information was filed against poor Baxter, oppressed, as he was, by age and infirmities. The accused man begged for time to prepare his defence. Jeffreys burst into a storm of rage; "Not a minute," he cried, "to save his life; I can deal with saints, as well as with sinners. There stands Oates on one side of the pillory, and if Baxter stood on the other, the two greatest rogues in the Kingdom would stand together." When the trial came on, at Guildhall, Baxter's friends, who loved and honored him, filled the court. At his side stood Doctor William Bates, one of the most eminent non-conformist divines. Two Whig barristers, of great note, Pollexpen and Wallop, appeared for the defendant. As Pollexpen began to address the jury, Jeffreys broke forth: "Pollexpen, I know you well, I will set a mark on you; you are the patron of the faction. This is an old rogue, a schismatical knave, a hypocritical villian. He hates the Liturgy, he would have nothing but long-winded cant, without book." And so Jeffreys went on and called Baxter a dog, and swore that it would be no more than justice to whip such a villian through the city. Wallop, the associate barrister, then interposed, but was quickly silenced. Then Baxter himself attempted to put in a word, but was overwhelmed by a torrent of abuse, calling Baxter a "snivelling Presbyterian," and fixing his savage eye on Bates, said: "There is a doctor of the party at your elbow, but, by the grace of God Almighty, I will crush you all." The noise of weeping was heard from some of those who surrounded Baxter. "Snivelling calves," said the Judge. He was sentenced to pay a fine of 500 marks, to lie in prison till he paid it, and be bound for good behaviour for seven years. It is said Jeffreys wished him to be whipped at the tail of a cart. The King remitted his fine, but he was kept in prison three years and six months. It is obvious that in the two noted instances, cited from many, the accused were punished not so much for what they had written as for the fact that they were in favor of a larger personal liberty than the tyrannical authorities would concede. Time will not permit further citations showing the history of the fight that has been going on many years for freedom of thought and speech. Compared with numerous instances in prior history, the treatment of Horne was moderate, yet a few years later it looked severe and outrageous. While Attorney-General Thurlow urged the pillory for Horne, Mansfield did not inflict it. Tracing English history in a sequential sense in our own Colonial and later history, we find this despotic tendency to suppress personal freedom. Not to cite cases in our Colonial history, we had a noted one as late as in 1854, when an attempt was made in Boston, through indictment, to punish Rev. Theodore Parker and Wendell Phillips for expressing their opinions in Faneuil Hall as to the Fugitive Slave Law, and the methods used to enforce it in the case of Burns, a fugitive slave, which aroused a wide interest in Boston and throughout the country. In this famous case, the Federal Judges, though eager for the indictment, seem to have got tired of the job, and upon a motion to dismiss the indictment upon technical grounds, promptly granted the motion.

The history of liberty, of freedom of speech, as known to English-speaking people, is the history of struggling oppressed human nature, whether in our own or in the mother country. It is the higher aspiration of manhood to live nearer to Him who is "the Author of Liberty."

When the War of the Revolution came to an end, the British constitution, though the Colonies were lost, remained substantially as we now know it, saving, of course, such amendments as a conservative progress has permitted. The American Republic was wisely established upon the basis of a written constitution guaranteeing liberty to its people. Let us hope that both nations may help by arbitrations, and in other ways, and not hinder what is best for humanity, and that both may become more and more, as the years go on, co-operative powers in promoting the best civilization in the world.

www.ingramcontent.com/pod-product-compliance
Lightning Source LLC
Chambersburg PA
CBHW021451090426
42739CB00009B/1723